D1541237

Animal Opposites

Jennifer Bové

muddy boots™

we jump in puddles

Guilford, Connecticut

Published by Muddy Boots
An imprint of Globe Pequot
MuddyBootsBooks.com

Distributed by NATIONAL BOOK NETWORK

The National Wildlife Federation © 2017 All rights reserved

Book design by Katie Jennings Campbell

Photo credits: Front cover photo © iStock.com/bzamora, back cover photo, page 1, and page 29 © iStock.com/tiverylucky, title page and page 2 © iStock.com/kugelblitz, page 4 © iStock.com/JohnPitcher, page 5 © iStock.com/zanskar, page 6 © iStock.com/Redders48, page 8 © iStock.com/Natural_image, page 9 © iStock.com/Freder, page 11 © iStock.com/svarshik, page 12 © iStock.com/IPGGutenbergUKLtd, page 13 © iStock.com/Evgeny555, page 14 © iStock.com/Betty4240, page 16 © iStock.com/Staselnik, page 17 © iStock.com/riderfoot, page 18 © iStock.com/pchoui, page 19 © iStock.com/edurivero, page 21 © iStock.com/compuinfoto, page 22 © iStock.com/BGreer, page 23 © iStock.com/GoodLifeStudio, page 25 © iStock.com/SteveOehlenschlager, page 26 © iStock.com/CreativeNature_nl, page 27 © iStock.com/Creative Nature_nl.

The National Wildlife Federation & Ranger Rick contributors: Children's Publication Staff,
Licensing Staff including Deana Duffek, Michael Morris & Kristen Ferriere,
and the National Wildlife Federation in-house naturalist David Mizejewski

Thank you for joining the National Wildlife Federation and Muddy Boots in preserving endangered animals and protecting vital wildlife habits. The National Wildlife is a voice for wildlife protection, dedicated to preserving America's outdoor traditions and inspiring generations of conservationists.

All rights reserved. No part of this book may be reproduced in any form or by any electronic or mechanical means, including information storage and retrieval systems, without written permission from the publisher, except by a reviewer who may quote passages in a review.

British Library Cataloguing-in-Publication Information available

Library of Congress Cataloguing in Publication Data available

ISBN 978-1-63076-292-6 (paperback)
ISBN 978-1-63076-293-3 (e-book)

™ The paper used in this publication meets the minimum requirements of American National Standard for Information Sciences—Permanence of Paper for Printed Library Materials, ANSI/NISO Z39.48-1992.

Printed in the United States of America

Contents

A mother elephant is *big*.
Her baby is *small*.

Big and small are opposites. Turn the page to explore more animal opposites.

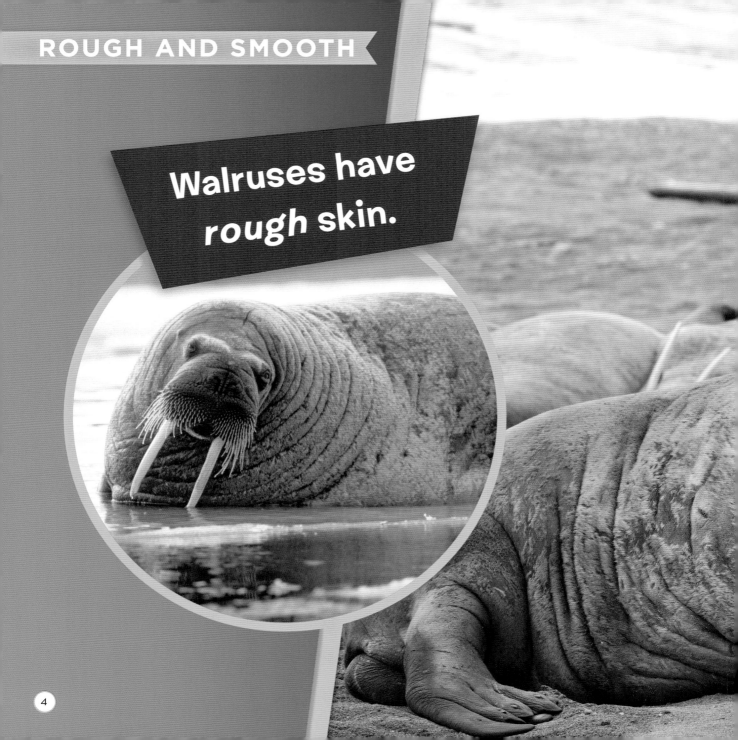

Walruses have **rough** skin.

A dolphin has *smooth* skin.

Cheetahs run *fast.*

A tortoise moves at a *slow* crawl.

Cougars have *long* tails.

A lynx has a *short* tail.

These pelicans have *open* bills.

These toucans have *closed* bills.

This prairie dog
is *in* its burrow.

These prairie dogs are *out* of their burrows.

A falcon flies
up in the air.

Mice walk *down* on the ground.

One macaw is showing its *front*. The other is showing its *back*.

Author: JENNIFER BOVÉ

Question: Have you seen a pair of animal opposites in the wild?

Answer: Last spring I saw a mother moose drinking from a river with her calf. The mom was huge and her baby was very small. It was amazing to imagine such a little calf growing up to be as big as its mother!

National Wildlife Federation Naturalist: DAVID MIZEJEWSKI

Question: Have you touched animals with opposite textures?

Answer: Yes! I get to handle all sorts of animals in my wildlife education work, from snakes which have wonderfully smooth, dry skin to foxes with fluffy, soft fur.

Illustrator: PARKER JACOBS *(Ranger Rick & Ricky characters)*

Question: Do you prefer to draw/paint in color or the opposite, black and white?

Answer: I love to draw and use lots of bright colors on many things. However, mostly I like to use black ink on white paper. It is the ultimate contrast (or opposite) that really conveys a visual message.